Aero Pictorials 4

Flying Leathernecks
in World War II

by

THOMAS E. DOLL

Art Work by W. M. Mulli‹

ISBN-0-8168-0312-9

LIBRARY OF CONGRESS CATALOG CARD NUMBER 79-123469
COPYRIGHT © 1971 AERO PUBLISHERS, INC.
ALL RIGHTS RESERVED
PRINTED IN THE UNITED STATES OF AMERICA

Aero Publishers, Inc.

329 Aviation Road
Fallbrook, California 92028

Foreword

Midway, Guadalcanal, Vella Lavella; names of places that before World War II few people knew existed. But in the years from 1941 to 1945 these remote islands became well known to almost every American old enough to comprehend the world around him. To those of us who served on these and the many others of islands in the Pacific, their names will not be forgotten nor the events that took place on these small but important landmarks.

This pictorial review of World War II United States Marine Corps aircraft will remind those of us that flew some of these aircraft in combat of events which not only affected our personal lives but may also have influenced the course of the war.

The photographs of the aircraft on Guadalcanal's Henderson Field will bring to mind special memories for we who served there; the primitive living and working conditions; the dust; the mud and the almost constant harassment by the enemy in the early days of our presence on the island. This was Guadalcanal.

Munda, Tarawa, Bougainville, Espiritu Santo, Peleliu, Iwo Jima, Okinawa; each a name, each a different place, each a poignant recollection.

The photographs within this book will give us all a nostalgic glimpse of an important time in our lives through the aircraft we flew and depended upon for our very existence. Although directed primarily toward the World War II naval aviation enthusiast, all who are interested in aviation will find this book both interesting and informative. This collection of photographs depicts a critical era in the history of United States Marine Corps aviation and that of our country.

Major General Marion E Carl, USMC
June 1970

A word about Major General Marion E. Carl, USMC.

General Carl, the Marine Corps' first air ace, who during the battle for Guadalcanal, downed 15 enemy aircraft, was twice awarded the Navy Cross, and finished World War II with 18 enemy aircraft to his credit, is widely known for the postwar records he established.

General Carl was born in Hubbard, Oregon, 1 November 1915. In 1938 he graduated with a BS degree in Mechanical Engineering from Oregon State College, where he was a member of the ROTC unit. He became a Marine aviation cadet in August 1938 and was designated a Naval Aviator, with the rank of second lieutenant in the Marine Corps on 1 December 1939.

As a section leader in Marine Fighting Squadron 221 during the Battle of Midway, he earned the Navy Cross in the attack against a vastly superior number of Japanese bomber and fighter planes. He earned a second Navy Cross at Guadalcanal.

Following WWII he became one of the first Marines to qualify in jets and made some of the first carrier landings and take offs with a Lockheed P-80 jet fighter. He became the first Marine helicopter pilot and earned a fourth Distinguished Flying Cross setting a world's speed record in the Douglas Skystreak in 1947. He later commanded the Marine Corps' first jet fighter squadron, VMF-122, at Cherry Point, N.C. and formed and led the first jet aerobatic team.

General Carl became the first Marine Aviator to earn the Octave Chanute Award for "notable contribution to the aeronautical sciences." He became the first Marine rocket pilot in 1953 and set an unofficial world's altitude record in the Navy's rocket powered Douglas Skyrocket, earning a fifth DFC.

General Carl commanded a Marine photographic squadron in Korea and served as Executive Officer of Marine Aircraft Group 11 in Japan. The General subsequently served in the following assignments: Wing Safety Officer; Commanding Officer; Marine Aircraft Group 33 and Assistant Chief of Staff, G-3, respectively, 1956 to 1958. Staff of the Air War College, Maxwell AFB, Alabama; Joint Chiefs of Staff; Headquarters USMC as Assistant Director and later Director of Aviation and as Assistant Deputy Chief of Staff for Air, 1959 to 1963.

In July 1963, he reported to the Hawaii based 1st Marine Brigade as Chief of Staff. Upon his promotion to Brigadier General in January 1964, he assumed command of the Brigade. General Carl was deployed to Okinawa with units of the Brigade early in 1965. In April and May of that year he placed units of the 1st Marine Brigade ashore in Vietnam at Phu Bai and Chu Lai. In August 1965, he returned to Vietnam as Assistant Wing Commander of the 1st Marine Aircraft Wing.

Following his assignment with the 1st MAW, the General then became Commander, Marine Corps Air Bases, Eastern Area; Commander, 2nd Marine Aircraft Wing and Commanding General, Marine Corps Air Station, Cherry Point, North Carolina.

As of 10 July 1970, General Carl has been assigned as Inspector General of the Marine Corps with offices at Headquarters Marine Corps, Washington, D.C. Major General Carl and his wife, the former Miss Edna Kirvin of Brooklyn, New York, have two children, Lyanne and Bruce.

Acknowledgements

The author wishes to express his appreciation to the following individuals and organizations who gave of their time, patience and energy to make this pictorial history of Marine Corps Aviation in World War II possible.

Major A. J. Bibee, USMC, (Retired).

Mr. Allan W. Cairncross, American Aviation Historical Society, Sydney, Australia.

Colonel F. C. Caldwell, USMC, Marine Corps Historical Branch.

Mr. Harry S. Gann, American Aviation Historical Society, Huntington Beach, Calf.

Mr. Rowland P. Gill, Marine Corps Historical Branch.

Mr. Thomas C. Haywood, Vice President, Flying Tiger Lines, Los Angeles, Calif.

Mr. B. R. Jackson, American Aviation Historical Society, Northridge, Calif.

Mr. M. J. Kishpaugh, American Aviation Historical Society, No. Hollywood, Calif.

Mr. C. L. Jansson, American Aviation Historical Society, Santa Ana, Calif.

Mr. William T. Larkins, American Aviation Historical Society, Pleasant Hill, Calif.

The staff of the National Archives & Records Center, Washington, D.C.

Dedication

This volume of the Aero Pictorial Series is respectfully dedicated to Orval A. Prevost, aviator, gentleman and friend.

Author's Note

This volume of the Aero Pictorial Series will present a pictorial review of United States Marine Corps aviation in World War II.

Beginning with the year 1940, we will examine the aircraft flown by the Marine Corps during the years so important to us all. From 1940 through 1945. The BG-1's, F3F's, F4F's, SBD's, TBF's, F4U's and many more will make their appearances on these pages enabling the reader to see the changes that took place in Marine Corps aircraft during the war years.

In addition, all but a few of the photos presented in this volume are actual Marine Corps airplanes photographed in their actual locales. Every attempt has been made to insure that squadron information, locality and dates are as accurate as humanly possible.

Because of the pictorial format of this volume, it cannot be thought of as an in-depth study of Marine Corps Aviation's activities during the Second World War. There have been many excellent books published covering that subject in detail. This is a visual study of one group's participation in a world wide struggle, it is a study of the machines flown by that group.

Thomas E. Doll

FLYING LEATHERNECKS
in World War II

1940

This year was one of promise for the Marine Air Force, new and faster airplanes were coming their way and talk of expansion was in the air. The war in Europe was beginning to have an influence on most everyone's thinking and the threat of Japan, more than ever before, kindered thoughts of how we'd measure up to the Japanese Air Force with our slower, wire braced biplanes.

In late 1940 the new airplanes began to arrive, the Douglas SBD-1. This sleek, all metal, low wing dive bomber marked the beginning of the end to the biplane era in the Marine Corps, the horizon looked brighter now than ever before.

GRUMMAN F3F-2
Captain Carson A. Roberts flying 1-MF-10. VMF-1, Quantico based, had 20 F3F-2's in 1940.   *(USMC)*

GRUMMAN F2F-1
Pugnacious looking little F2, shown here at Pensacola, was flown by fledgling Marine Corps aviators in 1940. (T. C. Haywood)

BOEING F4B-4
One of several Boeing biplanes flown by Marine aviation cadets at Pensacola, Florida in 1940. (T. C. Haywood)

BOEING F4B-4A
Taken over by the Navy, the Army P-12E's at Pensacola were designated -4A's and saw service as drones. This -4A, shown at Pensacola, was flown by Marine Aviation Cadets in training. (T. C. Haywood)

NORTH AMERICAN NJ-1
Three Pensacola based NJ-1's in formation being flown by Marine Aviation Cadets in 1940.   *(USN)*

DOUGLAS SBD-1
The first SBD delivered to the Marines in 1940 is shown here in its landing configuration on 2 August 1940.   *(USN)*

DOUGLAS TBD-1
At the time, 1940, the TBD-1 was regarded as the most streamlined and modern of all naval aircraft by the cadets at Pensacola. Many Marine cadets hoped to fly the TBD after completion of their training but unfortunately or fortunately for them the Corps only flew 1 TBD and then only for a short time in 1941.
(T. C. Haywood)

VOUGHT SBU-1
Marine Aviation Cadets in the air over Biou Grande, Louisiana in 1940.
(T. C. Haywood)

GRUMMAN F3F-2's
VMF-2 became VMF-211 in July 1941 then went on to make Marine Corps history during the defense of Wake Island in December 1941. (USMC)

GRUMMAN F3F-2
VMF-1 Grumman biplane ¾ rear view.

(USMC)

VOUGHT SB2U-1
Vindicator used by VMF-1 as a tow target airplane. Photo taken at St. Thomas, Virgin Islands. SB2U-1 had top speed of 250 mph, length of 34', span of 42' and was powered by a Pratt & Whitney R-1535-96 engine.

(L. McCallum)

SIKORSKY JRS-1
VMJ-1 amphib at Bourne Field, Charlotte Amalie, Virgin Islands. Marine Corps insignia just aft of number 4 of aircraft coding was applied in scarlet and gold. (USMC)

DOUGLAS R3D-2
VMJ-1 transport shown at Bourne Field, Charlotte Amalie, St. Thomas, Virgin Islands in 1940. (USMC)

GREAT LAKES BG-1
October 1936 photo shows Colonel Roy S. Geiger in the cockpit of his new command plane. The BG-1 served with front line Marine squadrons until the SBD-1 replaced them in 1940. *(USMC)*

DOUGLAS SBD-1
Marines were the first to receive new Douglas dive bomber in late 1940. This beautiful, sleek new craft was first of an excellent series of Douglas SBD's to see service with the Marine Corps. Shown at the factory is number 1 bird of Quantico based VMB-1. *(Douglas A/C)*

GRUMMAN F3F-2
Into the bay at San Diego on 21 February 1940. 2-MF-4 was leader of second section within squadron.
(A. J. Bibee)

CURTISS SOC-3
Squadron Commanders SOC taxis by Sikorsky JRS-1 at NAS North Island on 6 May 1940, fuselage coding is 2-MS-1.　　*(A. J. Bibee)*

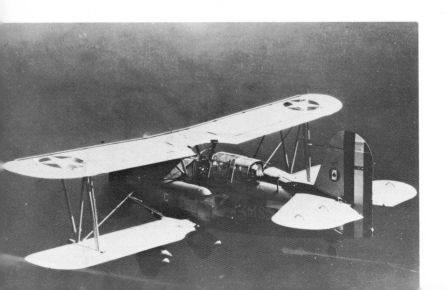

CURTISS SOC-3
Bad photographic example of a beautiful airplane. Seagull was thought by many to be one of the most attractive biplanes used by the Navy and Marines in the pre-war period. Fuselage coding is 2-MS-7.　　*(USMC)*

CURTISS SOC-3
"Ace of Spades" SOC at San Diego, California in 1940.   (W. L. Swisher)

CURTISS XSBC-4
Headquarters USMC XSBC-4 at NAS San Diego, California on 3 May 1939.
(A. J. Bibee)

GRUMMAN J2F-4
Number 5 bird of Utility 2, San Diego based 1940. Photo taken on 25 March '40.   (A. J. Bibee)

DOUGLAS R2D-1
Marine Paratroopers first trained in these all metal Douglas transports. Civil DC-2 was forerunner of famous "Gooney Bird" of pre-war, wartime and post-war fame. (USMC)

GRUMMAN J2F-2A
Photo taken prior to 19 March 1940, on that date an order was issued by the Bureau of Aeronautics directing that all aircraft taking part in the Neutrality Patrol were to carry the national insignia star on the forward section of the aircraft's fuselage. VMS-3, based at Charlotte Amalie, St. Thomas, Virgin Islands, participated in the Neutrality Patrol. (USMC)

GRUMMAN J2F-2A
Interesting shot of a Duck out of water. This J2F of VMS-3 was flown by 2nd Lieutenant Hains. (USMC)

GRUMMAN J2F-2A
Neutrality Patrol star adorns Grumman Ducks of Marine Scouting Squadron Three. "A" suffix on designation denoted addition of machine guns and bomb racks. VMS-3 had 9 J2F-2A's in 1940. (USMC)

1941

The year that brought great changes to the lives of many Americans was now at hand. Marine Aviation was making a slow but steady progress toward building the air force they had been promised by Congress in 1940.

The SBD-1 was now the front line dive bomber and the Grumman F4F-3 was gradually replacing the aging F3F-2 biplane fighter. Later in the year, the Brewster F2A-3 would enter squadron service thus eliminating all bi-wing fighters from first line duty in the Marine Corps.

When the Japanese struck Pearl Harbor on 7 December 1941, the Marine Corps Air Station at Ewa also fell victim to this well planned and precisely executed attack. Many planes were lost at Ewa but the most heroic page of Marine Corps history to come out of these early days of WWII was about to be written on a small strip of sand and rock called Wake Island.

Fighting 211 had only been on Wake a scant 5 days when the Japanese hit their airstrip; after the first raid of 8 December they found themselves down to only 4 operational airplanes and 8 pilots able to fly.

Despite almost insurmountable hardships, VMF-211 managed to keep their remaining F4's in the air, they flew against the enemy in a gallant but vain attempt to hold the island until relief could be sent. Relief never came.

On 22 December 1941, Wake Island fell to the Japanese, VMF-211 and the Marines on Wake had given their all. Captain Henry T. Elrod of '211 became the first Marine aviator to earn the Congressional Medal of Honor, though the award was not given until 1946 when the facts first became available. Captain Elrod lost his life on 22 December, shortly before the island fell.

VOUGHT SB2U-3
Vindicator of VMS-1 based at Quantico, Virginia. Overall light grey paint scheme began replacing colorful "peacetime" paint in February of 1941. Photo taken sometime between February and July 1941. On 1 July 1941 VMS-1 became VMSB-131. All USMC squadrons were redesignated on that date. *(USMC)*

GRUMMAN JRF-1
Command aircraft of the Commanding General, Second Marine Air Wing, Fleet Marine Force. *(Frank Shertzer)*

DOUGLAS SBD-1
VMB-2 Dauntless grabs a wire during carrier operations off West Coast 10 March 1941. *(USMC-USN-Nat. Archives)*

VOUGHT SB2U-3
In late 1941 VMSB-231 took delivery of 24 SB2U-3's. Shown in this photograph is one of the first -3's received by the Corps in early 1941.
(United Aircraft Corporation)

DOUGLAS R3D-2
Paramarines exit VMJ-152 transport in July 1941.
(Douglas Aircraft)

VOUGHT SB2U-3
Another Vindicator from VMS-1 taken after the squadron redesignation of 1 July 1941, VMSB-131 superceeded VMS-1. New designation system "told" complete wing, group, squadron data at a glance. Example: 131 breaks down thusly — 1 designates 1st Marine Air Wing, 3 designates 3rd Marine Air Group within the Wing and 1 designates the 1st squadron within the Group.
(USMC)

GLIDER SCHOOL
Flying a Schweizer LNS-1 glider, Lieutenant Colonel Guymon comes in low over a group of other Marine glider students on a field near Chicago, Illinois in 1941.
(USMC)

SCHWEIZER LNS-1
Six trainers were assigned to Marine Glider Group 71 at Page Field, Parris Island, South Carolina in late 1941. (USMC)

GLIDER TRAINING
Like giant birds these two Marine Corps gliders follow in the wake of an N3N towplane soon to be released to soar silently in the sky over South Carolina in 1941.
(USMC)

GRUMMAN F4F-3
New fighters for the Marines in the air on 28 May 1941. (USMC)

CURTISS SBC-4
The Second Marine Air Wing had 2 SBC-4's in 1941, this is the second of the two aircraft. (Frank Shertzer)

DOUGLAS TBD-1
VMS-2 received the one and only TBD-1 to serve with the Marine Corps on 26 March 1941. The San Diego based squadron gave up its TBD on 5 June 1941 when it was assigned to duty with VT-3 on the USS Saratoga CV-3.   (USN)

DOUGLAS SBD-2's
Fresh newly painted "grey ghosts" in flight over Southern California in 1941.   (W. T. Larkins)

DOUGLAS R4D-2
Marines used only 3 of the C-53 passenger version and Navy flew only 2 of the type. Navy types called -2, Marines, -3. Aircraft shown in photo is C-53 taken at Douglas Factory on 13 October 1941. (Douglas Aircraft)

VOUGHT SB2U-3
Marine Scouting Squadron 2 had 24 Vindicators at Ewa in 1941. In July they were redesignated VMSB-231.
(A. J. Bibee)

GRUMMAN F4F-3
The graveyard at the end of the line for planes of VMF-211 on Wake Island, 22 December 1941. Having fought until they were beyond salvage and repair, these are the remains of the Grumman Wildcats which defended Wake until they could fly no more against the overpowering foe.
(Japanese picture book-1943)

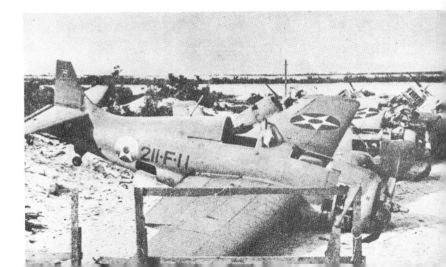

1942

Following Pearl Harbor we found ourselves in a more or less "hit and run" pattern of operations. The early '42 raids by Navy carrier based aircraft inflicted light to moderate damage on the Japanese but were actually blown out of proportion by exaggerated newspaper reports hoping to lift the morale of the American people, something we did need at the time.

While the fortunate few were hitting back at the Japanese, Marine Aviation personnel were hard at work trying to build up strength and train pilots and aircrewmen in order to take the offensive against the Japanese. By June, the Marine squadrons based on Midway Island would get that chance in a defensive sort of way.

After helping to stop the enemy at the Battle of Midway, Marine Aviation established itself on Guadalcanal and Operation Shoestring began. Every difficulty imaginable was put upon the Marines at Henderson Field, but with perseverance, teamwork and a bit of self-preservation inherent in us all, the island was finally secured.

NORTH AMERICAN SNJ-3 & CURTISS SBC-4
Two aircraft of the First Marine Aircraft Wing in flight in early 1942.   *(USMC)*

NORTH AMERICAN SNJ-3
Another VMD-2 aircraft at NAS San Diego on 15 April 1942. Markings on this J Bird are very unusual, basic airplane is natural metal, bands around fuselage and wings are Willow Green, red and white tail stripes adorn the rudder and huge oversized national insignia are apparent on the top of the orange-yellow wings and the side of the airplanes fuselage. As a rule SNJ's of this time period carried standard sized national insignia on the wings only, tail stripes were omitted. (A. J. Bibbee)

GRUMMAN J2F-5
Early in 1942 the Marines participated in the American Aviation Mission to the Carribean area.
(Grumman Aircraft Eng. Corp.)

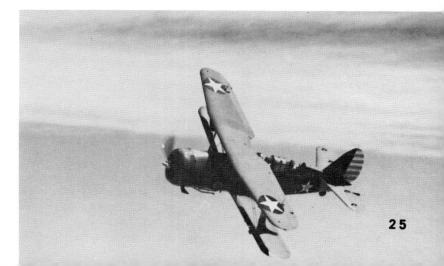

CURTISS SBC-4
VMO-151 flew these ancient Helldiver biplanes from the island of Samoa in April 1942. (USMC)

BREWSTER F2A-3
Unloading F2A from USS Kittyhawk at NAS Pearl Harbor, March, 1942. (USN-Nat. Archives)

GRUMMAN F4F-4's (USMC)

DOUGLAS R4D-1
Tail stripes and olive drab camouflage adorn this Marine Corps Gooney Bird in early 1942.   (Douglas Aircraft)

NAVAL AIRCRAFT FACTORY OS2N-1
Marines operated more of the NAF duplicates of the Vought OS2U than of the latter model. VMS-3 has 16 OS2N-1s and 2 OS2U-3s.
(National Archives)

VULTEE SNV-1
Training bird at NAS Corpus Christi, Texas in 1942. Student Marine aviators learned valuable lessons in the Vultee Vibrator throughout WW II.
(USN)

VOUGHT SB2U-3
VMSB-241 Vindicators take off from Midway Island 4 June 1942 to engage Japanese striking force off Midway Island during Battle of Midway. Although obsolete by 1942, the SB2U's of VMSB-241 fought well and gave great testimony to the dedication and skill of Marine Corps aviators.
(USMC)

GRUMMAN F4F-4
Refueled, rearmed and ready to go, VMF-211 Wildcat is being guided out of the revetment to the takeoff strip on Palmyra Island.
(USMC)

ESPIRITU SANTO
F4F-3P and J2F-5's can be seen being worked on beneath the sheltering palms of the Southwest Pacific, late 1942. Fuselage coding on F4F-3P reads "251-MO-5." (A. J. Bibee)

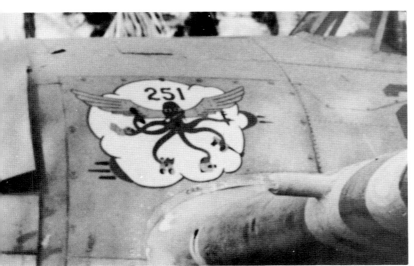

SQUADRON INSIGNIA VMO-251
VMO-251 was unusual combination to say the least. As their insignia illustrates they were photographers, mechanics, observers and fighter pilots. They flew regularly with Army B-17's from Tontouta and Espiritu, they also serviced the Army planes as well as Navy and Marine. On 2 January 1945 they were redesignated VMF-251 confirming what they knew for quite some time. Plane in photo is F4F-3P. (A. J. Bibee)

GRUMMAN F4F-3P
VMO-251 Wildcat on Kirby Schuessler Field, New Hebrides, 19 November 1942. Note squadron insignia on forward fuselage and shamrock just above fuel tank access panel.
(USN-Nat. Archives)

NORTH AMERICAN SNJ-4
Rare photo of VMF-112 SNJ-4 taken at Magenta Flight Strip near Noumea, New Caledonia, 12 November 1942. Pilot is Sgt. A. J. Bibee. Note twin caliber 30 machine gun in the SNJ's rear cockpit. (A. J. Bibee collection)

VOUGHT OS2U-3
VMS-3 Kingfisher on patrol over the Caribbean in July 1942. (USMC)

CONSOLIDATED PBY-5A
First plane to land on Guadalcanal's airfield 12 August 1942. PBY was flown by aide to Vice Admiral John S. McCain, Lt. William S. Sampson. Airstrip would later be named Henderson Field in honor of Major Lofton R. Henderson CO of VMSB-241 lost during the Battle of Midway, 4 to 6 June 1942. (USMC)

HENDERSON FIELD
SBD's, TBF's, PBY's, F4F's and Army B-17's shared Cactus Airfield with all its dust, mud and Japs in 1942. (USMC)

CACTUS OPEN AIR REPAIR SHOP
Marine planes on Guadalcanal await repair, pilots tents can be seen in the background. (USMC)

GRUMMAN F4F-4
Cactus Air Force Wildcat churns up the dust on Henderson Field, Guadalcanal as it takes to the air October 1942.
(USMC)

GRUMMAN TBF-1
VMSB-131 Avenger on Henderson Field December 1942, Capt. J. C. Aggerback in command. (USMC)

DOUGLAS SBD-3
VMSB-232 Dauntless on Henderson Field August 1942, Lt. Col. R. C. Mangrum in command. (USMC)

CONSOLIDATED PBY-5A
Major Jack Cram, personal pilot for General Roy S. Geiger, made an attack on a Japanese transport off Guadalcanal in his Catalina. The PBY, nicknamed the Blue Goose, carried two torpedoes on this run.   (Pratt & Whitney Aircraft.)
CONSOLIDATED PB4Y-1
VMD-254 Liberator on Henderson Field, Guadalcanal in 1942. This same plane, 31945, had 37mm cannon from a P-39 installed in its nose by VMD-254 personnel, see 1943.
(USMC)

1943

Marine Aviation continued its move over the blue Pacific, strike after strike was flown; the Russells, New Georgia, the Gilberts, the Carolines, names that would long be remembered by those who were there.

In November, Tarawa was taken and Marine Air began operations from its airstrip within days after the island was secure, thanks to the Navy's Seabees and the Army's Engineers. By this time Marine Aviation in the Pacific had grown into a tremendous force that along with its sister service, Navy Air, was equal to anything the Japanese could put into the air.

GRUMMAN F4F-3
Marine Wildcat in the air over MCAS Mojave, California on 25 March 1943.
(USMC)

DOUGLAS SBD-4
VMSB-233 workhorse, the Dauntless, being serviced on Henderson Field in January 1943. Handpainted aircraft number 41 and dirty appearance of SBD indicate that "fancy frills" were not the order of the day at Cactus.
(USMC)

GRUMMAN TBF-1
VMSB-131 "Turkey" waiting to be bombed up on Henderson Field, January '43. Squadron became 1st USMC torpedo-bombing squadron in June '43. Originally designated VMS-1 at Quantico, they flew SBD-1's in 1940 (USMC)

GRUMMAN F4F-4
Marine Wildcat on Henderson Field credited with 19 Japanese airplanes. Aircraft has had several pilots, but one crew-chief, TSgt. R. W. Greenswood. 9 February 1943. (USN - Nat. Archives)

VOUGHT F4U-1
First Marine squadron equipped with Corsairs, VMF-124, arrived on Guadalcanal 11 February 1943. (USMC)

CONSOLIDATED PBY-5A
VP-51 Catalina on Guadalcanal in 1943.   (USMC)

GRUMMAN TBF-1
VMTB-143 Avenger in flight in the Guadalcanal area June 1943. '143 ended war onboard USS Gilbert Islands CVE-107.   (A. J. Bibee)

37

VOUGHT F4U-1
VMF-124 Corsairs joining up with the photo plane in the Solomon Islands area on 22 April 1943. "Bubbles" leads the way. (A. J. Bibee)

GRUMMAN F4F-4's
Guadalcanal based Wildcats in flight May 1943. (A. J. Bibee)

DOUGLAS R4D-1
Henderson Field plays host to "Margie" and the "Texas Tramp" during stopover in 1943. (USMC)

CONSOLIDATED PB4Y-1
VMD-254 Liberator flying to Espiritu Santo in early 1943. A 37mm cannon was built into the nose of this airplane by VMD-254 personnel. The cannon was a fixed forward firing weapon "liberated" from a US Army P-39. (A. J. Bibee)

CONSOLIDATED PB4Y-1
VMD-254 photo Liberator over Espiritu Santo. New Hebrides 29 May 1943. Squadron was first to penetrate Truk area when photo Lib of 254 photographed the Puluwat Group on 26 January 1943. (A. J. Bibee)

NORTH AMERICAN SNJ-4
The PB4Y's pilots of VMD-254 used this SNJ to keep their hand in at single engine aircraft flying. It was also used to augment the training of aerial photographers. Inexperienced photographers trained in this plane before being assigned to a photo crew. Photo was taken on 6 June 1943 in the Espiritu Santo area.

(A. J. Bibee)

GRUMMAN F4F-4
Guadalcanal based Wildcat cruises over part of the Slot in May 1943. In April of that year, Lieut. James E. Swett shot down 7 Japanese planes in 15 minutes while flying and leading a four plane division of F4F-4's.
(A. J. Bibee)

GRUMMAN F4F-4
Replacement aircraft on way to add to the roster of birds on Guadalcanal. In 1943, the Marines continued to operate from Henderson Field by intercepting Japanese planes & ships coming down the Slot. Air units also escorted bombers flying up from Guadalcanal to attack airfields on New Georgia and Vila-Stanmore on the Southern tip of Kolombangara.
(A. J. Bibee)

DOUGLAS SBD-4
Over Guadalcanal on way to Munda.
(USMC)

LOCKHEED-VEGA PV-1
VMF (N)-531 was first Marine Corps night fighter unit. First "kill" of squadron was made on 15 November '43 when Captain Duane Jenkins shot down a Japanese Betty bomber as it headed for a naval task force in the company of five other Bettys.
(A. J. Bibee)

GRUMMAN TBF-1's
Marine "Turkeys" in flight over the Mojave Desert in mid-1943. (USMC)

NORTH AMERICAN PBJ-1
VMB-413 made the first PBJ raid in the Pacific when they hit Rabaul on 17 March 1944. VMB-413 was commissioned at Cherry Point on 1 March 1943.
(USMC)

DOUGLAS BD-2
Marines flew both the BD-1 (A-20) & BD-2 (A-20A) in limited numbers for target towing and general utility work.
(USMC)

BREWSTER SB2A-4
Pictured at Cherry Point on July 13, 1943, this re-
claimed Dutch bomber was used in training by
VMF (N)-531, first Marine night fighter squadron.
(USMC)

CURTISS SNC-1
St. Louis, Mo. built SNC at Cherry Point 13 July 1943.
Several advanced trainers were used by the Marine
Corps as liaison planes and glider tugs.   (USMC)

BREWSTER SB2A-2
The Buccaneers used by the Marines in 1943 for training purposes still had the instrument panels inscribed in Dutch.
VMF (N)-531 flew the SB2A-4 at MCAS Cherry Point in July 1943.   (USN)

BEECH GB-2
MCAS Cherry Point had 2 Staggerwings in its Base Air Detachment in 1943. *(USMC)*

GENERAL MOTORS (EASTERN DIVISION) FM-1
VMF-114, 115, 218, 225 flew the GM version of the Grumman F4F-4 Wildcat in 1943. *(USMC)*

HOWARD GH-2
Used as ambulance by Marines, the GH-2 was similar to the civil DGA-15. Marines also flew the -1 and -3 models.
(Harry Thorell)

BEECH JRB-1
Personal aircraft of Major General A. A. Vandegrift, Commanding General of 1st Marine Division. Photo taken at Essendon Airport, Melbourne, Australia, 6 July 1943. Two stars & 1st Division insignia adorn olive green and light grey Beech.
(USMC)

DOUGLAS SBD-4
"Flying Goldbricks" of VMSB-243 fly over 2 tiny islands in the Pacific which they help to guard. Relative size of islands may be seen by comparison of structures on them. *(USMC)*

VOUGHT F4U-1
Headquarters Squadron 31 Corsair at Cherry Point 13 July 1943. *(USMC)*

RUSSELL ISLANDS FIGHTER STRIP
VMF-123 F4U-1's taxi out on to the runway prior to making a sweep to the north of the Russell Islands. Note unusual placement of star & bar national insignia on the tops of both wings of the Corsairs in the photograph. Standard placement called for one insignia on the top of the port wing and one on the bottom of the starboard wing. (USMC)

VOUGHT F4U-1
Nine days after Munda fell on 5 August '43, VMF-123 & 124 were operating from the airstrip built by the Navy's Seabees. (USMC)

GRUMMAN F6F-3
F6 possibly from the USS Barnes CVE-20 taxis down the runway on Betio Island, Tarawa Atoll. Barnes and Sangamon CVE-26 were the only escort carriers to operate F6's in this action. The F6 above carries CVE ID letter on its fuselage while aircraft from the bigger CV's taking part in this operation did not use letter ID symbols. Bloody battle wrote stirring page in Marine History.   (USMC)

A CAP FOR A JAP — VMF-214 The Black Sheep
To solve a shortage of baseball caps, traditional wear in the South Pacific for Marine airmen, members of Major Gregory "Pappy" Boyington's fighter squadron in October offered to down an enemy aircraft for every cap sent them by players in the World Series. Twenty caps arrived from the St. Louis Cardinals in December. These 20 original members of the Black Sheep accounted for 48 Japanese planes, the large percentage since the offer went out for the baseball caps in October. They are shown, wearing their caps on the wing of "The bent wing bird," the F4U-1 Corsair. Vella Lavella, 1943.   (USMC)

1944

By this time we enjoyed a pretty moderate degree of air superiority, of course after the June air actions at the Battle of the Philippine Sea our air supremacy was never questioned. The actions of that year; Kwajalein, Truk, Eniwetok, the Marianas, the Philippine Sea battles, Saipan, Guam, Tinian, Peleliu, Leyte, Mindoro, would find Marine Air playing important parts. Marine squadrons would also operate from these islands, sometimes even when the fight was still in progress.

DOUGLAS SBD-6
VMSB-231 Dauntless, 13 May '44 over
Majuro Atoll, Marshall Islands.
(USMC)

VOUGHT F4U-1
Red outlined national insignia is
sported by this Corsair taking off
from the airstrip on Bougainville in
January 1944. Red outline was sup-
posed to be deleted and replaced by
blue outline by this time but appar-
ently this one got by. Army P-39 Aira-
cobra sits in background of photo.
(USMC)

VOUGHT F4U-1
Corsair at rest on Torokina Point, Bougainville fighter strip. VMF-115, 211, 212, 215, 216, 217, 218, 223, 251 and 321 operated from Bougainville in 1944.   (USMC)

LOCKHEED-VEGA PV-1
Night fighting Ventura bomber on Bougainville, January 1944.   (USMC)

GRUMMAN TBF-1
Stripped of guns, this Avenger carried over 3,000 lbs. of cargo for Marines on Bougainville.   *(USMC)*

VOUGHT F4U-1
Off for Rabaul: this pilot lifts his Corsair off the fighter strip at Empress Agusta Bay on a raid to Rabaul. Gear is just starting to come up.
(USMC)

DOUGLAS SBD-5's
VMS-3 Dauntlesses, in their low visibility grey and white paint scheme, fly anti-submarine patrol in the Carribean area. Squadron was decommissioned in May 1944. Major Christian C. Lee was last CO. (USMC)

VOUGHT F4U-1
100 mission VMF-111 "Devil Dog" Corsair. The same engine carried her on all of them plus many other hops, reconnaissance, search and test. (USMC - Larkins)

CURTISS R5C-1's
On the line in two tone camouflage paint, Marshall Islands 1944.   (USMC - Larkins)

PIPER NE-1
"Grasshoppers" on Pavuvu in the Russell Islands, August 1944. USS RuPage prepares for disembarkation in background.
                                                                                    (USMC)

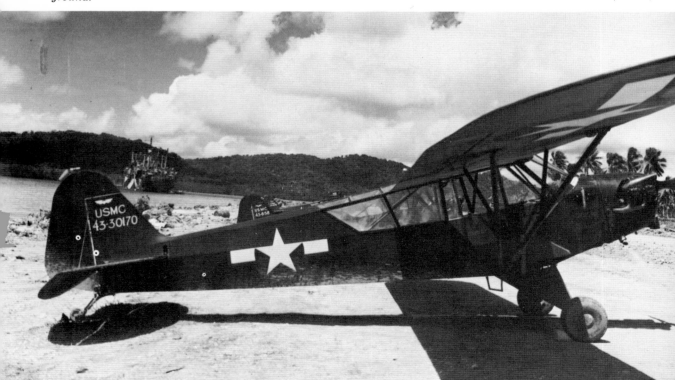

GENERAL MOTORS (EASTERN DIVISION) TBM-3
VMTB-232 Avenger at Ulithi in 1944. This squadron started out in 1941 as VMSB-232, it was originally VMB-2 prior to the 1941 squadron redesignation.   (USMC)

GRUMMAN TBF-1C

First American plane to land on Saipan, bearing wounded gunner for medical treatment. Plane is from USS Wasp CV-18, Air Group 14, squadron is VT-14.

(USMC)

VOUGHT F4U-1

Triple O of VMBF-331 in flight October 1944. VMBF-331 designation assigned only 2 months, in December '44 designation reverted back to VMSB-331 and unit once more operated SBD's. Eleven mission marks adorn Corsair just below cockpit canopy.

(USMC)

CURTISS SB2C-3
4th Marine Air Wing Helldivers over the Central Pacific.   *(USMC)*

GETTING TO BE A HABIT
113 missions for this VMSB-231 SBD-6.   *(USMC)*

ENLISTED GUNNERS TAKE A BREAK
Rear seat gunners of VMSB-231 outside their ready room on Majuro Atoll, mid-1944.

VOUGHT F4U-1
Famed "Ace of Spades" squadron flew Corsairs for a short time, October '44 to December '44 and were designated VMBF-231 during that time period. Rare photo shows "Ace of Spades" insignia on F4U just forward of canopy. (USMC)

GRUMMAN F6F-3N
VMF (N)-534 night fighter on Orate Field, Guam. On 4 August 1944, VMF-216, 217, 225 and night fighting 534 took off from the USS Santee CVE-29 and landed on Guam ending a 13 year absence of Marine Corps aviation on the island.
(USMC)

VOUGHT F4U-1D's
"U Birds" of Marine Air Group 21 lined up on Guam's Orate Field.   (USMC)

VOUGHT F4U-1D
Crew chief gets good view of airfield activity on Guam, November '44.   (USMC)

GRUMMAN TBF-1C
First plane to land on Peleliu, out of gas, made forced landing. Landing took place on D plus 4. (USMC)

GRUMMAN F6F-5N
VMF (N)-541 Hellcat on Peleliu September 1944. (USMC)

GRUMMAN F6F-5N's
Servicing VMF (N)-541's night fighting Hellcats on Peleliu.   (USMC)

VOUGHT F4U-1D's
Major Robert F. Stout's VMF-114 Corsairs take off from Peleliu's airstrip, October '44.   (USMC)

OVER RABAUL
PBJ-1D makes for home after a strike on Matupi Island guarding the entrance to Rabaul Harbor.   *(USMC)*

NORTH AMERICAN PBJ-1D
The Flying Nightmares, VMB-413, flew heckling missions against Rabaul in early '44.   *(USMC)*

NORTH AMERICAN PBJ-1D
Two F4U's escort this Mitchell bomber on a practice flight near MCAS El Centro, California.　　　　(USMC)

NORTH AMERICAN PBJ-1D
Tri-color Mitchell bomber at Ewa.　　　　(USMC)

TIMM N2T-1
Col. Valentine Gephart, CO of Air Base 2, NAS North Island, flys molded plywood trainer over San Diego, California.

(Jansson - Larkins)

1945

Two full scale amphibious operations occurred this year, both of which involved Marine Corps aviation, they were Iwo Jima and Okinawa. Marine squadrons rolled up some of their highest scores during these engagements plus Marine units onboard carriers participated in the carrier strikes on Formosa, Hong Kong, Cam Ranh Bay, Saigon and Tokyo.

The first all-Marine carrier, the USS Block Island CVE-106, went into action in early 1945. By May the Corps had 3 additional aircraft carriers to call their own; the USS Gilbert Islands CVE-107; the USS Cape Gloucester CVE-109 and the USS Vella Gulf CVE-111.

When the war came to a halt in August, Marine Aviation had more than proven itself to be highly skilled in all phases of the game. From a small "stepchild" of naval aviation in 1940 they had developed into a large, highly organized, mobile and powerful weapon by 1945. Marine Air had come of age during WW II and today it continues to grow.

Today the emphasis is on the future and this is as it should be for it's where we will be spending the rest of our lives, but we should not neglect our heritage. Marine Aviation has a proud heritage, one that began with dedicated, professional and resourceful men and that is being carried onward by people just as devoted as the pioneers of the past.

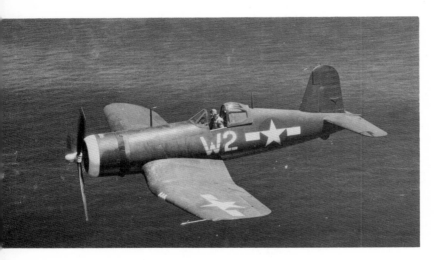

VOUGHT F4U-1
Ewa, Hawaii based Corsair in flight. Ewa's aircraft were assigned letters V, W, Z, for ID purposes in the Hawaiian area, September 1945.

(USMC)

MARINE FIGHTER ESCORT
VMF-124 F4U-1D's from the USS Essex CV-9 escort a VT-83 TBM-3 from the same carrier on a strike against Formosa, 3 January 1945. This strike was the first in which Marine pilots fought from a carrier deck. When returning home, Lt. Col. William A. Millington, Jr., CO of VMF-124, shot down a twin engined fighter (Nick) to become the first Marine flier in history to shoot down an enemy aircraft while operating from a carrier. *(USMC)*

VOUGHT F4U-1D
Both VMF-214 and 452 served on-board the USS Franklin CV-13 in 1945. On 19 March 1945 the Franklin was severely damaged with great loss of life. *(USN)*

DECK SCENE USS BUNKER HILL CV-17
VMF-221 and 451 operated from CV-17 during assault on Iwo Jima, 19 February 1945. They flew F4U-1D's. *(USN)*

VOUGHT F4U-1D
VMF-217 Corsair being positioned on USS Wasp CV-18 in early 1945. (USN)

VOUGHT F4U-1D
Major Hanson of VMF-112 is shown taking off from the USS Bennington CV-20, 17 February 1945 for strike on Toyko.
(USN - Nat. Archives)

GRUMMAN-F6F-5N
VMF (N)-511 night fighting Hellcat on deck of USS Block Island CVE-106, 1st Marine carrier, February 1945. (USMC)

GENERAL MOTORS (EASTERN DIVISION) TBM-3
Avenger of VMTB-233 is secured to flight deck of Block Island, February 1945. (USMC)

GRUMMAN F6F-5N
The "Hangar Queen" gets the go-ahead on Block Island, 10 May 1945. (USMC)

GRUMMAN F6F-5N
"Butch" after hitting barrier on Block Island. Hellcat carries clever ID symbols for Block Island on tail surfaces, white block and black I. Small letter M signifies Marines. *(USMC)*

GENERAL MOTORS (EASTERN DIVISION) TBM-3's
Avengers from the USS Cape Gloucester CVE-109, fly over Saddle Island near Shanghai, 29 July 1945.
(USN - Nat. Archives)

VOUGHT F4U-1D
Take off action onboard USS Cape Gloucester CVE-109 another all-Marine carrier then operating in the East China Sea. Squadron is VMF-351, same squadron that participated in "Project Danny." "Danny" was project conceived in 1944 to utilize "Tiny Tim" rockets against Nazi V-1 rockets being used against England. VMF-511, 512, 513 and 514 plus VMO-351 were attached to this project and were due to go to Europe when the project was abandoned due to the shortage of "Tiny Tim" rockets. VMO-351 redesignated VMF-351, February '45.   *(USMC)*

VOUGHT F4U-1D
Lt. Col. D. K. Yost, USMC, takes off from USS Cape Gloucester CVE-109 in the East China Sea, 1945.
(USN - Nat. Archives)

GENERAL MOTORS (EASTERN DIVISION) FM-2
FM-2 from Marine Corps training unit catches wire but still hits the barrier on the USS Solomons CVE-67 in May 1945.
(USN - Nat. Archives)

CURTISS SB2C-4's
VMSB-244, The Bombing Banshees, Helldivers over Davao, Mindanao, June '45.
(USMC)

70

DOUGLAS SBD-5
VMSB-241 dive bomber on Luzon. (USMC)

VOUGHT F4U-1's
VMF-222 planes carry USN Seabee insignia as tribute to the unit for its outstanding work on Samar Island in the Philippines. (USMC)

FIGHTING 222's "Seabee" INSIGNIA
Seabees-Leatherneck squadron insignia is admired by Lieutenant Commander H. Koopman, CB unit executive officer;
Commander B. M. Bowker, CB commanding officer and Marine Major R. T. Spurlock, commanding officer of the Flying
Deuces, VMF-222. All 222 planes carried the insignia.
(USMC)

GENERAL MOTORS (EASTERN DIVISION) FM-2
First fighter plane to land on Iwo Jima's Motoyama Airfield # 1, 29 February 1945. Aircraft is from the USS Shamrock
Bay CVE-84, squadron is VC-94.
(USMC)

VOUGHT F4U-1's
Corsairs that flew escort for Fleet Admiral Chester Nimitz when he visited Iwo Jima in March 1945.   (USMC)

GOODYEAR FG-1D's
Lined up on Iwo with Mount Surabachi in the background. Planes are stopping over for fuel on way to Okinawa. FG was built by Goodyear on subcontract from Vought.
(Clay Jansson)

CONSOLIDATED OY-1
"Lady Satan" with 3 bazookas under each wing. VMO-4 & 5 served on Iwo during battle.　　　　　　(USMC)

GENERAL MOTORS (EASTERN DIVISION) TBM-3
VMTB-242 "Turkey" taking off for anti-submarine patrol around Iwo Jima, March 1945.　　　　(USMC)

NORTH AMERICAN PBJ-1H
Lt. Col. Jack Cram's night fighting, rocket firing VMB-612 flew 251 sorties from 10 April to 28 July 1945. Targets were located in 83 of these missions. Squadron record for this period: 53 ships damaged, 5 sunk. Shown here is the #9 plane of the squadron about to go in on a rocket run.
(USMC)

VOUGHT F4U-1D
VMF-312 Corsair on Okinawa's Kadena Airfield, April 1945.
(USMC)

MARINES HAVE LANDED
1st Lt. Fred M. Borwell, USMC, (in plane) was the second pilot to land on Okinawa's Kadena Airfield, 9 April 1945. On wing is 1st Lt. William J. Dempsey, USMC. They are both members of VMF-312.   (USMC)

VOUGHT F4U-1D
T/Sgt. Frank Burke pushes 500 lb. bomb out to VMF-312 fighter plane on Okinawa. VMF-312, "Day's Knights", was commanded by Major Richard M. Day, USMC.   (USMC)

VOUGHT F4U-1D
Napalm laden birds of VMF-322 on Kadena Airfield, Okinawa, April 1945.   *(USMC)*

CURTISS R5C-1
TAG transport on Okinawa, April '45.   *(USMC)*

CHECK IN TIME ON OKINAWA
Crewmen of the "Red Devils", VMTB-232, check in at Kadena Airfield, Okinawa, 4 May 1945. From left; Sgt. James T. Cantwell, radio-gunner, Cpl. Walter W. Kline, turret gunner. (USMC)

MARINE TORPEDO BOMBING SQUADRON 232
Section of VMTB-232 approaches southern Okinawa to make bomb run against Japanese installations. (USMC)

GENERAL MOTORS (EASTERN DIVISION) TBM-3
VMTB-232, "The Red Devils", aircraft lines up for a bombing run over Okinawa, April 1945.   (USMC)

VOUGHT F4U-4's
VMF-212 and 223 were the first USMC squadrons to receive -4 Corsairs on Okinawa, 15 May 1945.   (USMC)

GRUMMAN F 7F-3N
Sleek, powerful Tigercat arrived too late to see combat on Okinawa, but did provide security patrol. Photo taken on Okinawa's Chimu Airstrip, 20 August 1945.
(USMC)

GRUMMAN F 6F-5P
VMD-354 camera equipped Hellcat on Guam.
(Clay Jansson)

CONSOLIDATED PB 4Y-2
Privateer from Ewa in flight, April 1945.   (USMC)

NORTH AMERICAN PBJ-1J's
Tri-color B-25J's armed and ready to go, May 1945.   (USMC)

CURTISS R5C-1's
Transport Air Group (TAG) Commandoes on Ulithi, squadron is VMR-952.

(USMC)

GRUMMAN J2F-5
Over Falalop, Ulithi 5 April 1945.

(USMC)

CANADIAN CAR & FOUNDRY COMPANY SBW-3's
VMSB-245 Helldivers on Falalop Island, Ulithi, 30 May 1945.

(USN - Nat. Archives)

GRUMMAN F 6F-5N's
VMF (N)-541 night fighters on Falalop Island, Ulithi, 30 May 1945.   *(USN - Nat. Archives)*

NORTH AMERICAN SNJ-3
Overall Glossy Sea Blue paint scheme adorns Marine Corps Texan, 1945.   *(USMC)*

VOUGHT F4U-1's
On the line at MCAS Santa Barbara, California, March 1945.   *(USMC)*

VOUGHT F4U-1
Corsair covered with snow at MCAS Mojave, California, a desert air station.   *(USMC)*

MARTIN JM-1
Tow target plane painted orange-yellow for maximum visibility during gunnery practice.   *(W.T. Larkins)*

NORTH AMERICAN SNJ-5
MCAS El Toro "J Bird" with El Toro insignia on forward fuselage.   *(USMC)*

BREWSTER F3A-1 & GOODYEAR FG-1
MCAS El Toro, California Corsairs, late 1945. F3A was late model F4U-1 built under license by Brewster Aeronautical Corp. FG-1 (G-237), was fixed wing version of F4U-1 built under license by Goodyear.

(A. J. Bibee)

CURTISS SB2C-4
Marine "Beast" over Yap Island, 28 August 1945.

(USMC)

CURTISS SB2C-4's
Helldiver line up at Ewa, Hawaii, 1945.

GRUMMAN F6F-5's
Hellcats from Ewa on a training mission, September 1945.   (USMC)

MATSUYAMA AIRFIELD, FORMOSA
Major Peter Folger and Captain Dick Johnson are met by curious Japanese as they descend from their Block Island TBM-3, the first American account to land on Formosa. Landing was at Matsuyama Airfield to arrange deliverence of prisoners, September 1945.   (USMC)

MATSUYAMA AIRFIELD, FORMOSA
Captain Johnson stands on the wing of his TBM relaying radio message to the Block Island 50 miles at sea, telling of progress in negotiations at the airfield.
(USMC)

VOUGHT F4U-1D's
Marine Air Group 22 Corsairs being lined up outside hangar at Omura Naval Air Base, Japan soon after their arrival in September 1945.
(USMC)

91

CURTISS SB2C-4

Lieutenant F. C. Lambert, USMCR, on patrol over Jaluit Atoll, 23 October 1945. Japanese cruiser Kasima was then preparing to evacuate 911 Japanese nationals from this former Japanese capitol of the Marshalls. The USS Thornhill DE-195 provided escort and can be seen in the background. (USMC)

AIRFIELD SCENE — NAN YUAN, CHINA
Tigercat, Hellcat, Warhawk and Mustang at Nan Yuan, Peiping, China, 10 December 1945.   (USMC)

CONSOLIDATED OY-1
1st Marine Air Wing "Grasshopper" on patrol near Chinwangtao, China, December 1945.   (USMC)

FROM PEARL HARBOR TO TOKYO BAY, PROUDLY SHE WAVED.

Index

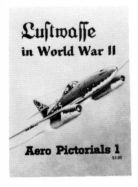
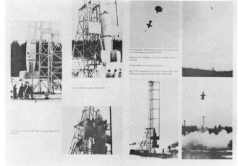